30 DAY DEVOTIONAL

Let's Chat

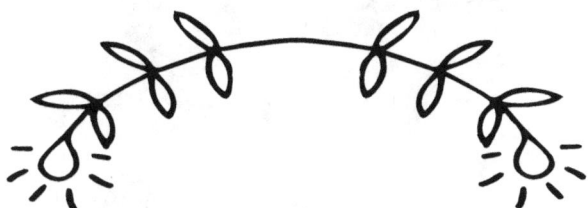

CONVERSATIONS
WITH MOTHERS
& DAUGHTERS

30 DAY DEVOTIONAL

Let's Chat

CONVERSATIONS WITH MOTHERS & DAUGHTERS

SINIKKA WAUGH

Let's Chat
Conversations with Mothers and Daughters
30-Day Devotional

ISBN # 978-0-578-82422-2

Published by:
Sinikka L. Waugh
Indianola, Iowa

All Scripture quotations, unless otherwise indicated, are taken from the King James Version. Public Domain.

Scripture quotations marked (NIV) are taken from the Holy Bible, New International Version®, NIV®. Copyright © 1973, 1978, 1984, 2011 by Biblica, Inc.™ Used by permission. All rights reserved.

Scripture quotations marked (NKJV) are taken from the New King James Version®. Copyright © 1982 by Thomas Nelson. Used by permission. All rights reserved.

Scripture quotations marked (NRSV) are taken from the New Revised Standard Version Bible, © 1989 the Division of Christian Education of the National Council of the Churches of Christ in the United States of America. Used by permission. All rights reserved.

Book/Cover Design: Tamara Parsons

Dedication

To Anne Marie, Ashley,
and Anne,

in joyful memory of
conversations that have been,

in quiet tribute to
conversations that
will never be,

and in blessed assurance of
conversations that will
take place in Glory.

Table of Contents

Welcome!

IN THE FOLLOWING PAGES you'll find a 30-day devotional workbook designed to bring women closer to God and to each other in their daily conversations.

While the messages were originally written to spark discussion between mothers and daughters, I invite you to go through this workbook with a mother, daughter, grandmother, aunt, niece, or any other sister-in-Christ as a great way to explore your faith together on topics–the struggles, the joys–that we frequently encounter as women. Sometimes we know these things in our hearts, but we don't always get the opportunity to chat through them together. This workbook is designed to help us do just that. These lessons should take between 5 and 15 minutes each day, though I imagine you'll find that some discussions could go on much longer if you let them.

THE STRUCTURE: Each daily devotional has a Title, a handful of Bible Verses, and some Thoughts to Consider. Read these together, then proceed to the workbook section where you'll find questions for each of you to answer (in a box on each page), more scripture passages for further reading, and a couple more discussion questions. Each daily devotional closes with a prayer.

Each Week begins with an introductory paragraph to help foster your discussions and to help explain some of the inspiration behind this workbook. In general, the workbook is designed to prompt conversations around communication, salvation, living a life of salvation, and rest and peace.

Several of the devotions are accompanied by coloring pages or illustrations that allow you to doodle or color as you chat. Many of us have experienced the profound conversations that can take place in the car, when we're not directly looking at each other, and you may find the same thing can happen when you color while chatting.

HOW TO: This workbook is meant to be completed in the order in which it's written, but if you miss a day, you can pick up where you left off the next time you come to it, or skip it and come back to it another day. It's totally up to you! I encourage you to read the Bible passages and commentary together first. Then, ask each other the questions designed for Mother and Daughter, making time to chat for a bit. Next, take turns reading and reflecting on the Bible verses. Then spend a few minutes talking through the discussion questions–use all the time you need there! When you're ready, wrap up with the closing prayer. The workbook is designed to spark conversation, so you can use it over and over again. As we change and grow, as we experience different stages of our lives, our answers in this workbook might change, too. It can be fun to revisit our answers and see how we've changed–and how we've stayed the same!

THE SOURCE: The Thoughts to Consider, questions, and prayers are all mine. They are prayerful musings to help you in your conversation. God gets all the glory if something touches you and inspires you; I take all the blame if I've missed the mark somewhere or represented something poorly. The Bible verses are generally taken from the New Revised Standard Version (NRSV), and also occasionally from the King James Version (KJV), New International Version (NIV), Good News Translation (GNT), and New King James Version (NKJV). The translation is always indicated.

I pray that this devotional workbook will bless you and your relationships with the very special women in your life.

Sincerely,

Sinikka

He has made
everything
beautiful
in its time

Ecclesiastes 3:11

Talking

I'LL NEVER FORGET THE DAY, when my oldest daughter was nine, riding in the back of the car one Saturday morning while we were running errands, and she asked, "Mom, we're going to have dark days, aren't we?" I was startled at first by her question because I wasn't sure where she was coming from, but as we talked it through, she pointed out, "Well, someday I'm going to be a teenage girl, and you're going to be the mom of a teenage girl. And from what I hear, teenage girls and their moms often have dark days, don't they?" After a quick prayer about how to answer her, peace came over me as I offered the approach that God had laid on my heart, "Well what do you think about this: how about we decide now to love each other through the dark days and just keep talking to each other?" She reflected for a moment and replied, "That sounds like a good idea. So, what's for lunch?"

Creating a relationship between mothers and daughters where communication can continue to flow is absolutely critical.

Some of the devotionals in this workbook are meaty and heavy. Some of them are much lighter. Some of the discussion questions are light and fun, some of them probe a little deeper. I hope you are able to foster an open, easy conversation together, taking cues from some of this week's topics.

Reflect a bit on your communication: Do you both use the same types of communication approaches? Do you tell stories together? Are you good listeners together? Do you have conversations or one-way monologues? Look for the languages that you each speak—your conversational styles, times of day when your communication is most effective, and even your love languages. Use this week to focus on intentional conversations.

In the Beginning, God

Bible Verses:

Genesis 1:1-2 (KJV)[1] In the beginning God created the heaven and the earth.[2] And the earth was without form, and void; and darkness was upon the face of the deep. And the Spirit of God moved upon the face of the waters.

John 1:1-4, [...] 14 (NRSV)[1] In the beginning was the Word, and the Word was with God, and the Word was God.[2] He was in the beginning with God.[3] All things came into being through him, and without him not one thing came into being. What has come into being[4] in him was life, and the life was the light of all people. [...][14] And the Word became flesh and lived among us, and we have seen his glory, the glory as of a father's only son, full of grace and truth.

Thoughts to Consider:

In the Beginning, before time began, God is and was and will always be. God is the eternal one. He was not created or formed, but by Him all things were created. God the Father, Jesus Christ the Son, and the Holy Spirit were all in existence before time began. Three persons in one God have always been and will always be. God is constant and unchanging. He created all things and all beings. Nothing exists without God's hand of creation. He made us! Our finite minds struggle to understand an infinite God, and so He came to live among us so that we could see Him, know Him, and understand Him better. Let's talk a little about eternity and what that means.

Question for Mother to answer:

Can you think of a time when a moment seemed really long at the time but looking back, it's merely a "blink of an eye"?

Question for Daughter to answer:

What's something in your life that just "is," and you accepted that it was here before you were born, and that will always just "be"–as if it feels somewhat permanent?

Verses to explore together

- Isaiah 40:28
- Hebrews 13:8
- Psalm 90:2
- Revelation 1:8

Discussion Questions together:

1. Lots of families play pretend. In a way, the act of getting down on the floor and connecting with kids is a little bit like what God did for us. What games did we play together when you were smaller?

2. God is unchanging. As humans we change. Parents learn to care for and connect with their children in different ways, and children grow and learn. But sometimes there are some "constants" in our character that help us understand God's permanence. What's something that has been pretty "constant" for us?

Closing Prayer:

Lord, thank You for creating the heavens and the earth. Thank You for creating all things, including us. Eternity is a hard concept to grasp. Thank You for giving us ways to understand You better. This day, help us seek out things in Your creation to be grateful for, and help us find ways to help others know You, too. Amen.

Beloved,
let us love
one another,
because love is
from God

1 John 4:7a (NRSV)

God is Love

Bible Verses:

1 John 4:7–8 (NRSV)[7] Beloved, let us love one another, because love is from God; everyone who loves is born of God and knows God. Whoever does not love does not know God, for God is love.

1 John 3:1 (NRSV)[1] See what love the Father has given us, that we should be called children of God; and that is what we are.

Thoughts to Consider:

God has loved us with an everlasting love. God, who is the very essence of love, has shown us His love by sending His Son to show us the way to heaven. Love comes from God, because love is His very nature. We can love each other because God has taught us what love looks like. God also calls us His children! What a wonderful expression: to love with a parent's love! Some families use the words "I love you" to express love. Others show their love through actions (working outside the home to provide for the family, giving gifts, putting food on the table, washing and folding clothes, helping with the chores or homework, hugs, or just sitting together quietly). Let's talk about love a little.

Question for Mother to answer:

How would you describe the feeling of love you have for your child(ren), from the very moment they were born until today?

Question for Daughter to answer:

How have you seen your family demonstrate love for each other over the years?

Verses to explore together

- Jeremiah 31:3
- Deuteronomy 7:9
- John 3:16
- 1 John 4:7–21

Discussion Questions together:

1. The love that a parent has for their child can give us a hint about what God's love looks like. What parent-child examples in real life or in movies and stories can you think of that show a parent's love?

2. Even more than any earthly examples we can think of, God's love is eternal and boundless and entirely unchanging. What might it look like to have a love that never changes and that's always abundant?

Closing Prayer:

Lord, thank You for creating the heavens and the earth. Thank You for creating all things, including us. Eternity is a hard concept to grasp. Thank You for giving us ways to understand You better. This day, help us seek out things in Your creation to be grateful for, and help us find ways to help others know You, too. Amen.

God is love

God Knows You

Bible Verses:

Psalm 139:1 (NRSV)[1] For it was you who formed my inward parts; you knit me together in my mother's womb.

Psalm 139:15–16 (NRSV)[15] My frame was not hidden from you, when I was being made in secret, intricately woven in the depths of the earth.[16] Your eyes beheld my unformed substance. In your book were written all the days that were formed for me, when none of them as yet existed.

Thoughts to Consider:

The God of the Universe knows you and loves you. Sometimes it's a little scary to be known; other times it's wonderful. It can be fun when a friend finishes our sentences because they know us so well. When we fear that someone can guess what we're thinking, that can be unpleasant. Sometimes we feel insufficient. We fear we're not smart enough, or kind enough, or talented enough. God knows us, and He loves us simply because He made us. God knows every hair on your head. He knows every thought you have ever had and will ever have. He knows what makes you tick. He knows what ticks you off. He knows your intentions and your actions. He knew you from before you were born, because He created you. He carefully, and wonderfully, wove together the strands of DNA that would become you. Let's talk about being known.

Question for Mother to answer:

What are some things you know about your daughter, perhaps things you knew about her before she knew them herself?

Question for Daughter to answer:

What are some of the characteristics you share with your parents (it could be eye color or hair color, your personality or your love of music–anything you can think of that you have in common with them)?

Verses to explore together

- Ephesians 2:10
- Luke 12:7
- Jeremiah 1:4–8

❀ · ❀ · ❀ · ❀ · ❀ · ❀ · ❀ · ❀

Discussion Questions together:

1. A quick Google search will show you that the average human has between 90,000 and 150,000 strands of hair on their head. What does it mean to you to know that God knows each strand of hair? What does that say about how much you are worth to Him?!

2. The prophet Jeremiah had a moment when he thought he was too young and not well-spoken enough to speak the Word of the Lord. How did God's response in Jeremiah 1:7–8 give you encouragement?

❀ · ❀ · ❀ · ❀ · ❀ · ❀ · ❀ · ❀

Closing Prayer:

Lord, thank You for the time and care and love with which You created us. Thank You for being patient with us when we fear we're not good enough, and for reminding us that You created us exactly the way we were meant to be, and that You love us. Thank You for being with us as we live out each day of our lives. Help us today to be who You created us to be, and to give You all the glory for Your creation. Amen.

But I Don't Always Like the Way I Look

Bible Verses:

Ecclesiastes 3:11 (KJV) He hath made every thing beautiful in his time.

Psalm 139:14 (NRSV)[14] I praise you, for I am fearfully and wonderfully made. Wonderful are your works; that I know very well.

Thoughts to Consider:

Society puts so much pressure on us to look a certain way that we tend to hide our imperfections under layers of makeup or clothes that cover the extra Christmas goodies we ate. They even sell clothes that have the "right" shapes already built into them so we can look the way we're "supposed" to look so no one will know we're not perfect. But God doesn't ask us to be perfect or to look like anyone else. He has always known you, and always loved you, even before you were born. He created you exactly the way you are—your hair color, your eye color, the fingers on your hands, the toes on your feet. He made you exactly the way you were supposed to be. He loves you for how tall you are today and how tall you'll ever get. He loves you, because He created you. God is perfect and makes no mistakes. Let's talk about external beauty.

Question for Mother to answer:

Did you ever feel the pressure of trying to look just the way society says we should look? What ways have you found to deal with that pressure?

Question for Daughter to answer:

What does "beautiful" look like to you?

Verses to explore together

- 1 Peter 3:3–4
- Song of Solomon 4:7
- Matthew 6:28–30

Discussion Questions together:

1. As little girls, many of us play dress-up. We dress up in fancy dresses or put on pretty shoes or beads. What are some of your favorite memories of dress-up?

2. Scholars say the Song of Solomon is an allegory for how much God loves His people and how much Christ loves His bride ("the church"). The language is very different from what we might use today, but how does it make you feel to hear someone say to you, "you are altogether beautiful"?

Closing Prayer:

Lord, thank You that we are fearfully and wonderfully made. Thank You that You love us and that You make everything–us included–beautiful in its time. Lord, sometimes it's hard to feel beautiful when the noisy voices of the world around us make us feel insecure. Thank You for specific verses in the Bible that we can lean on when we're feeling unlovely on the outside. We know that beauty comes from You. Help us to continue to shine from the inside out with Your love. Amen.

God Sees You

Bible Verses:

Genesis 16:13 (NRSV) So she named the Lord who spoke to her, "You are El-roi"; [God who sees].

Thoughts to Consider:

Sometimes we feel unseen or invisible. "No one understands me," or, "No one even pays attention to me," are thoughts we've shared from time to time. But those thoughts are from the Enemy trying to steal our joy. The truth is, God knows you, God loves you, and God sees you. The setting for today's scripture is from the story of Hagar. A slave in the house of Abram and Sarai, (before they became Abraham and Sarah respectively). Hagar had been harshly treated by Sarai. She had run away and was pregnant and alone in the wilderness. Can you imagine how lonely she felt? She stopped (I can imagine how she fell to the ground in exhaustion and thirst and sadness and loneliness) by a spring of water, which she then named "The Well of the Living One who sees me." At this lonely moment of her life, she encountered God. He found her, and He saw her. The Hebrew word Hagar used for "the one who sees me" is "El Roi" (pronounced el raw-ee). This verse in Genesis is the only time the name "El Roi" is used, but it's not the only time in the Bible where we read about how God sees us. What a comfort to know that even in our moments of deepest loneliness, God sees us. Let's talk about feeling 'unseen'.

Question for Mother to answer:

Can you share a story about a time you felt lonely or unseen? How did the situation change?

Question for Daughter to answer:

What kinds of situations make you feel unseen or lonely? What do you do when you encounter those situations?

Verses to explore together

• Isaiah 41:10   • Psalm 68:4–6
• Psalm 25: 14–17

Discussion Questions together:

1. For little kids, hide and seek can be kind of scary unless you know someone is actually looking for you. What stories do you remember of playing hide and seek as a kid?

2. In today's society with so many electronics "connecting" us to each other, experts say we're seeing a rise in individual loneliness. How can you help someone else feel less lonely this week?

Closing Prayer:

Lord, thank You for seeing us. Thank You for Your promise to find us and be with us when we're lonely and afraid. Thank You for the refreshing water that comes from the well, which You have placed for us when we're just at the end of our own ability. Thank You for finding us and seeing us. Help us to also see others who are lonely and to refresh them with a comforting word. Amen.

God Desires a Relationship with You

Bible Verses:

1 Timothy 2:3–4 (NRSV) God our Savior,[4] who desires everyone to be saved and to come to the knowledge of the truth.

John 15:15 (NRSV)[15] I do not call you servants any longer, because the servant does not know what the master is doing; but I have called you friends, because I have made known to you everything that I have heard from my Father.

Thoughts to Consider:

It's hard to imagine that the God who created the universe desires to have a relationship with us, but it's true. He created us in His image. He wants to be our God, and He wants us to be His people.

He wants us to know and understand His love for us, and to spend time in daily conversation with Him. God is not some distant, far-off being. He is here, present, and desiring a close relationship with you. Spending time together is an important part of any relationship. In the book of Luke, when Jesus was criticized for spending time with sinners, He tells a parable about a shepherd who leaves his flock of 99 to go after one sheep who has wandered away. That's the way God is with us. He seeks after us. He finds us to bring us back closer to Him. Let's talk about relationships.

Question for Mother to answer:

Grandparents, aunts and uncles, and cousins sometimes live far away, and we don't get to see them very often. Are there any relatives that seemed far-away and distant to you when you were growing up?

Question for Daughter to answer:

What do you know about your extended family today? Think about your grandparents, aunts, uncles, cousins, etc. With whom do you have a close relationship? Why do you suppose that's true?

Verses to explore together

- Genesis 5:1
- Luke 15:1-7
- Leviticus 26:12
- 2 Peter 3:9
- John 1:12
- 1 Thessalonians 5:9-10
- John 3:17

Discussion Questions together:

1. Sometimes in family, we love and accept each other even if we don't live close to each other. What kind of work, time, and effort does it take to build a close relationship with someone who loves you?

2. What relative or family friend can we bless today by giving them a phone call or sending them an email or a text?

Closing Prayer:

Lord, thank You for desiring a relationship with us. You know us, You see us, You love us, and You want us to connect with You and spend time with You. Lord, thank You for chasing after us and seeking us out so we can grow closer to You. Help us find ways to draw closer to You today. Amen.

We rejoice
in hope
of the glory
of God

Romans 5:2

God Has a Great Plan for You

Bible Verses:

Jeremiah 29:11(NRSV) For surely I know the plans I have for you, says the Lord, plans for your welfare and not for harm, to give you a future with hope.

Romans 8:28 (NRSV) We know that all things work together for good for those who love God, who are called according to his purpose.

John 10:10b (NRSV) I came that they may have life, and have it abundantly.

Thoughts to Consider:

God has a plan for you. His sees you, He loves you, He knows you, and He seeks you out because He has chosen you. You are a child of God, and His plan for your life is to give you hope and a future. He wants to give you life—not just average, ho-hum, mediocre life, but abundant life! How cool is that? As humans, we don't understand God's plans and God's ways as He does, so it's easy to get discouraged when things seem hard or when bad things happen to good people, but God promises us that all things work together for good! And God is good, all the time. The life He promises for us isn't in material blessings of money and fame, more clothes, more shoes, or more things; it's the hope of eternal salvation and forever with Him. It's relentless love, overflowing joy, and peace that surpasses all understanding, and it's available to us today if we choose Him. Let's talk about plans for a moment.

Question for Mother to answer:

How did your life turn out differently than you'd planned when you were my age? How have you seen God at work in the unfolding of your life?

Question for Daughter to answer:

What kinds of plans and hopes and dreams do you have for your life?

Verses to explore together

- Philippians 4:19
- Lamentations 3:25–26
- Philippians 1:6
- Jeremiah 29:11–14
- Psalm 138:8

❀ · · · ❀ · · ❀ · · · ❀ · · · ❀ · · · ❀ · · · ❀ · · · ❀ · · · ❀

Discussion Questions together:

1. Sometimes things that seem difficult in the moment wind up working out to a better end. What examples of this can we come up with from our own lives or from the lives of those around us?

2. God promises a life of abundance. What do you picture when you hear about abundance? Can you share moments when you've caught a glimpse of the overwhelming, cup-running-over, abundant joy God promises us when we rely on Him?

❀ · · · ❀ · · ❀ · · · ❀ · · · ❀ · · · ❀ · · · ❀ · · · ❀ · · · ❀

Closing Prayer:

Lord, thank You for Your promise of abundance. Thank You for choosing us, for loving us, and for drawing us closer to You. Lord, help us not be distracted by our human desire for material things but rather to focus on a life of abundant goodness through You. Amen.

For God so
loved the world
that He gave
His one and only
Son that whoever
believes in Him
shall not perish
but have
eternal life

John 3:16 (NIV)

Salvation

AS A MOM, OF COURSE I CARE ABOUT MY DAUGHTERS'
health and wellness and if they grow up to be capable, confident,
and contributing members of society. Of course, I want to make
sure they are eating healthy foods, that they have a warm place to
sleep, and that their education is helping to stretch their minds
and maximize their talents.

But more than any of that, I want to know their souls are
redeemed. Nothing in my daughters' lives is more important
than their salvation.

But sadly, salvation not something we talk about all the time. It
seems somehow relegated to Sunday mornings or maybe a brief
conversation at dinner time or evening tuck-in. So I designed this
workbook to foster conversations about *salvation.*

What is it? Why do we need it? How can we grasp it? How do we
claim it?

Nothing that I ever say or do will be more important than pointing my loved ones toward their redeemer and Savior–He who is their only hope of eternal life with God.

Reflect a bit on your own salvation journey. Perhaps now is the time to ensure your own eternal peace. Perhaps you and your daughter have already claimed the saving and redeeming grace of Jesus Christ, and this week could be used to reflect on how you can share the Gospel so you can bring others to eternal Life. Use this week to focus on salvation.

Separated from God

Bible Verses:

Romans 3:23 (NRSV) Since all have sinned and fall short of the glory of God.

Isaiah 59:1–2 (NRSV) See, the Lord's hand is not too short to save, nor his ear too dull to hear.[2] Rather, your iniquities have been barriers between you and your God, and your sins have hidden his face from you so that he does not hear.

Thoughts to Consider:

God is perfect. In His perfect state, He cannot tolerate sin. Sin cannot exist in His presence. Picture the brightest, most perfect light you can imagine. In its presence, darkness does not and cannot exist. Darkness and light can't be in the same place at the same time. But we, in our human nature, have the darkness of sin– every one of us. From the very first sin in the garden of Eden (in Genesis 3 when both Eve and Adam ate fruit of the tree of the knowledge of good and evil even though God had commanded them not to) until now, human kind has been separated from God. Big sins, little sins: there's no difference in God's eyes. And because God is just, if we sin, we cannot be with God. The ancient Israelites had a practice of offering sacrifices to atone for (or make amends for) their sins. Even those sacrifices did not take away the sin, but they covered over them. God gave the Israelites a way to stay close to Him even when they had sinned because He desires a relationship with his people. In an even greater way, God gave us the gift of His Son to take away our sins so we can dwell in His presence. Tomorrow's devotional will talk more about salvation, but for a moment, let's talk about the darkness of separation.

Question for Mother to answer:

Have you ever been separated from someone you love? Can you share the story of how you felt and what happened next?

Question for Daughter to answer:

Imagine being in total darkness for a few moments, what thoughts would go through your head?

Verses to explore together

- Romans 5:12
- Ephesians 2:1–3
- John 8:34
- John 3:3

- 2 Thessalonians 1:8-10
- Isaiah 53:6
- Galatians 5:19-21
- 2 Timothy 3:2-4

❀ · ❀ · ❀ · ❀ · ❀ · ❀ · ❀ · ❀

Discussion Questions together:

1. It's tempting to judge other people's sins as worse than ours. Can we think of times when we've brushed off our own sins as not as bad as someone else's? What do today's verses say about that?

2. Words from Galatians 5:20–21 like "jealousy," "anger," "strife," "quarrels," and "envy" sound like things we do every day. Can we think of examples?

❀ · ❀ · ❀ · ❀ · ❀ · ❀ · ❀ · ❀

Closing Prayer:

Lord, help us to recognize our own sins so we can confess them to You and claim Your gift of Christ Jesus as our savior. Amen.

The Price of Sin is Paid

Bible Verses:

Romans 6:23 (NRSV) For the wages of sin is death, but the free gift of God is eternal life in Christ Jesus our Lord.

Romans 5:8 (NRSV) But God proves his love for us in that while we still were sinners Christ died for us.

John 3:16 (NRSV) For God so loved the world that he gave his only Son, so that everyone who believes in him may not perish but may have eternal life.

Thoughts to Consider:

God loves you so much that He sent His Son to die for your sins. Christians often use language like "the blood of Christ shed for the forgiveness of sins," or "washed clean in the blood of the Lamb." These phrases can sound confusing or even gross if we don't understand them. God loves us and wants to have a relationship with us. But because we are sinners, our sin is like a darkness that separates us from the light of God. Before Christ, closeness with God came from following the book of the law carefully and by making sacrifices through a priest when the law was broken. But God wanted more for us. He sent his Son Jesus Christ to live on this earth–a perfect God-Man. The Messiah was fully human and fully God, born of the virgin Mary. In His perfect God nature, Jesus Christ did not sin. And as a man, he was put to a horrific death on a cross, even though He had done nothing wrong. He died, was buried, and on the third day, He rose again. He conquered over death and ascended into heaven. All of these things happened in accordance with the scriptures of the Old Testament. All of them happened because God loves us and wanted to save us for eternity. And all of them would have happened for just you–that's how much God loves you. The death of Jesus Christ was the sacrifice that paid for our sins. The sins had to be paid for because God is just and righteous. We cannot pay for our own sins because as humans we can't make ourselves clean; God didn't have to pay for our sins because He did not commit them. Only Jesus Christ could bridge the gap between humans and God by taking on the punishment of those sins on our behalf. God does not sell salvation; He does not barter with it; He does not ask us to earn it; He simply offers it as a gift that we can accept or reject. Let's talk about gifts.

Question for Mother to answer:

We celebrate the birth of Christ by giving gifts every year during the Advent season and Christmas. What are some of your favorite gift memories—either gifts you gave or gifts you received?

Question for Daughter to answer:

What are some of your favorite Christmas stories, songs or Christmas traditions? Why are they your favorites?

Verses to explore together

- 1 Timothy 2:5
- John 14:6
- John 1:29
- Luke 1:26-45
- Luke 2:8-20
- Matthew 2:1-12
- Isaiah 7:14
- Isaiah 9:6-7
- Micah 5:2-3

|||||||||||||||||||||||||||||||||||||||||||||||||||||||||||||||||||

Discussion Questions together:

1. Salvation is a pretty heavy topic. If you've accepted the gift of Jesus' saving grace, will you share your salvation story?

2. What kinds of opportunities do we have to share the story of salvation with others?

|||||||||||||||||||||||||||||||||||||||||||||||||||||||||||||||||||

Closing Prayer:

Lord, thank You for Your saving grace. Thank You that You loved us enough to die for us. Thank You that You took on the punishment of my sins and that You conquered over death so I can accept Your love and spend eternity with You. I confess my sins and my inability to be in Your presence without the sacrifice paid by Jesus Christ. Thank You for this gift. I know I can't earn it, and I can't pay for it. I know I'm not worthy, but You, Lord, have loved me and chosen me and saved and redeemed me, and it is because of You that I can stand boldly before the throne of God. Thank You. Lord, help me live a life that shows others Your saving grace. Amen.

For whosoever
shall call upon
the name of
the Lord shall
be saved

Romans 10:13

Confess Him and Live

Bible Verses:

Romans 10:13 (NRSV) For, "Everyone who calls on the name of the Lord shall be saved."

Romans 10:9–10 (NRSV) [9] Because if you confess with your lips that Jesus is Lord and believe in your heart that God raised him from the dead, you will be saved. [10] For one believes with the heart and so is justified, and one confesses with the mouth and so is saved.

John 14:6 (NRSV) Jesus said to him, "I am the way, and the truth, and the life. No one comes to the Father except through me.

Thoughts to Consider:

The words are neither complicated nor magical. But they are powerful. The scene: a concert with a popular Christian artist performing. The lyrics and melody move the audience. Some lift their hands in worship. Others close their eyes as they sing along.

Still others sway where they stand, touched by both the music and the message. A preacher takes the mic. His message is succinct and clear: "God loves you; we are all sinners and cannot reach God on our own. God loves you so much, He sent His Son to take away your sins. Christ lived and died to pay the price of your sins and rose again in triumph over the grave. Your sins are forgiven if you simply accept this gift and confess Him as Lord." Tears flow freely around as hearts are convicted by God's love. The preacher speaks again, "If your heart has been moved this day, and if you have not yet accepted Jesus as your Lord and Savior, will you come, right now, and pray this simple prayer?" A handful of individuals walk forward to pray the simple words. Still others remain in their places yet pray the same words, and their lives are changed forever. Let's talk about life-changing moments.

Question for Mother to answer:

Can you describe any of the life-changing moments in your life? What happened? Where were you? How did they change you?

Question for Daughter to answer:

Who have been some of the influential people in your life so far who have made you stop and think about what you believe? What kind of impact have they had on you?

Verses to explore together

- John 20:31
- 1 Thessalonians 4:13–18
- John 5:24
- Ephesians 2:8-10
- Romans 1:1-6
- 1 John 1:9

Discussion Questions together:

1. Have you ever been to an event that included a moment where people were invited to give their lives to Christ? Can you describe it? An important piece is the confession. We need to believe with our hearts and confess with our mouths that Jesus is Lord. What does it mean to "confess with our mouths"?

2. Many people seem to live as if they think they can earn grace or earn salvation; they think if they're just good enough, they'll go to Heaven. But the Bible teaches us that salvation is a free gift from God. It cannot be earned. How does that impact how you talk about and practice your faith in God?

Closing Prayer:

Lord, I know that I have sinned and that I don't measure up to Your glory. I understand that the cost of my sin is death. I know that Jesus' death on the cross paid for my sins and the slate is wiped clean. I repent of my sins and I confess Jesus Christ as my Savior and Lord of my life. Thank You for Your love. In Jesus' Name, Amen.

God Is Our Protector

Bible Verses:

Psalm 18:1–3 (NRSV) [1] I love you, O Lord, my strength. [2] The Lord is my rock, my fortress, and my deliverer, my God, my rock in whom I take refuge, my shield, and the horn of my salvation, my stronghold. Lord, who is worthy to be praised, so I shall be saved from my enemies.

Romans 8:38–39 (NRSV) [38] For I am convinced that neither death, nor life, nor angels, nor rulers, nor things present, nor things to come, nor powers, [39] nor height, nor depth, nor anything else in all creation, will be able to separate us from the love of God in Christ Jesus our Lord.

Thoughts to Consider:

Imagine this: The deck is clearly stacked against the underdog. It's one of those 1980's video games where all the bad-guys are coming at the hero–little combinations of dots on a screen, they're moving fast and coming closer. They're bigger; they're stronger; they have more troops and more powerful weapons. It looks like it's going to end badly for the hero. But, wait, what's that? The hero has a God-bubble around him? With God as his protector, the enemies keep bouncing off and falling away, while the hero remains unharmed and triumphant.

Here's another one. Again, the deck is stacked against the heroine. She's tiny compared to the giant monster coming at her. The dragon breathes fire and threatens to destroy her. But with the flick of a wrist, she launches her most powerful weapon–the name of God–and the dragon is vanquished.

Okay, so with apologies to Space Invaders and Super Mario Bros, video games aren't the perfect analogy for God's power, but it's thought provokingto knowthat God is our protector and our defense. Let's talk about games and defenses.

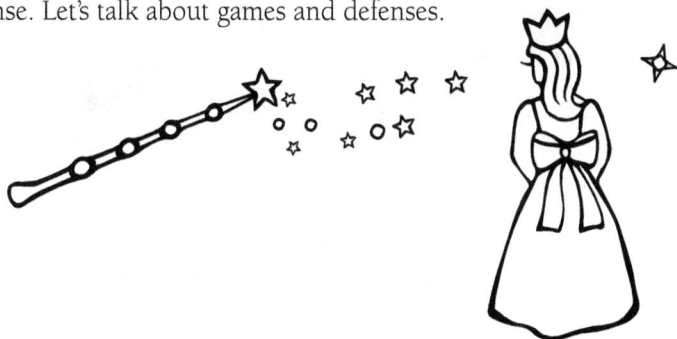

Question for Mother to answer:

What are some of your favorite games? What memories do you have of playing those games?

Question for Daughter to answer:

What are some of the most popular video games you're aware of today? Have you played them? What are some of the tools of defense in those games?

• •

Discussion Questions together:

1. When facing Goliath, David shows us how, with God on our side, we will beat the strongest enemy. How does that apply to our lives today?

2. What does it mean to you to know that nothing is impossible for God?

• •

Verses to explore together

- 1 Samuel 17
- 2 Corinthians 4:8-9
- Psalm 28:6-8

- Jeremiah 32:17
- Jeremiah 32:27
- Isaiah 41:10

- Matthew 19:26
- Luke 18:27
- Luke 1:37

Closing Prayer:

Lord, thank You for being our protector. Thank You that nothing can separate us from Your love. Help us live lives that show we trust in You. Amen.

The Lord is
my strength
and my
shield

Psalm 28:7a

What About the Tough Times?

Bible Verses:

Romans 8:18 (NRSV) I consider that the sufferings of this present time are not worth comparing with the glory about to be revealed to us.

Psalm 34:19 (NRSV) Many are the afflictions of the righteous, but the Lord rescues them from them all.

Thoughts to Consider:

A lot of people believe that just because I'm a Christian, or just because I believe in God, that means that bad things won't happen to me or to people I love. It means I won't be sad or broken hearted. It means I won't get sick or injured. It means I'll have all the money and stuff I want at my fingertips and that I'll always get my way. That's just not true. Thank goodness God loves us too much to give us everything we think we want! God doesn't promise an easy road. He doesn't promise there won't be trials or pain. In fact, He pretty much assures us that we will have tough times (See John 16:33), but He also promises that He is with us in the moments when we're hurting or scared. He promises we will not be defeated, because He is on our side. He promises this present pain is NOTHING compared to the glory we will know in Him. In Revelation 21:4, we read about a time when there will be no more crying and no more pain, and we have that to look forward to! An easy analogy for today's verse from Romans 8 is to think about pregnancy and childbirth. Swollen feet during pregnancy are a minor nuisance, but they're nothing compared to the swelling of love in your heart that happens when the baby is born. For the vast majority of women, childbirth is a painful experience. But that moment of pain is forgotten. It's nothing at all compared with the joy of holding that newborn baby. Let's talk about that.

Question for Mother to answer:

What stories can you share of pregnancy or childbirth?

Question for Daughter to answer:

Can you share a time when you went through something tough, but you knew that someone was there for you so you weren't alone?

Verses to explore together

- John 16:33
- Revelation 21:4
- James 1:2-4
- Psalm 46:1
- Isaiah 12:2

Discussion Questions together:

1. When have we seen God at work through tough moments in our lives?

2. Oftentimes, we have the opportunity to show God's love to others by being there for them during times of trouble. How can we show God's love to those we know today?

Closing Prayer:

Lord, thank You for promising to be with us during the times of trial and pain. Thank You for the promise of a future with no tears. Help us be Your hands and feet to those who need comfort. Amen.

God Heals the Broken-Hearted

Bible Verses:

Psalm147:3 (NRSV) He heals the brokenhearted and binds up their wounds.

Psalm 34:18 (NRSV) The Lord is near to the broken-hearted, and saves the crushed in spirit.

Thoughts to Consider:

Have you ever had a broken heart? They can be pretty awful. Hollywood shows them with tears, a sense of emptiness, comforted by hugs, piles of tissues, and pints of ice cream—eaten with a spoon, right out of the container. Make that two spoons, because so many of us find that at the saddest moments of our lives, we take comfort in knowing that someone is there with us. Broken hearts feel especially lonely, and we don't want to be left by ourselves. God promises to be near us in our times of sorrow and broken heartedness. He promises He will be near to us. He will hear us, we can share our sorrows with Him, and He will lighten our load. But God promises more than ice cream—even more than chocolate chip cookie dough ice cream! God promises to heal the broken-hearted and to bind up their wounds. Let's talk about how heart-ache heals.

Question for Mother to answer:

Can you share any stories of broken hearts in your life? What brought you comfort?

Question for Daughter to answer:

What kinds of things make you sad? What brings you comfort?

Verses to explore together

- Ecclesiastes 3:1–15
- Psalm 73:26
- 1 Peter 5:7
- Psalm 9:9
- Psalm 30:5
- Matthew 11:28-30

❀ · ❀ · ❀ · ❀ · ❀ · ❀ · ❀ · ❀

Discussion Questions together:

1. Ice cream seems to be a pretty common comfort food. What's your favorite ice cream flavor? Have you ever turned to ice cream (or some other food) for comfort? How did that turn out?

2. Has there ever been a time when you've been there for a friend who was sad? What did you do? How did it turn out?

❀ · ❀ · ❀ · ❀ · ❀ · ❀ · ❀ · ❀

Closing Prayer:

Lord, thank You for loving us so much that You can see right into our hearts, know our hurt, and provide comfort and healing when our hearts ache. Thank You for teaching us to love so that we can provide comfort to others when they are sad. Lord, help us to remember to draw on Your strength, and to help others see Your comforting love. Amen.

I can do all things through Christ who strengthens me

Philippians 4:13

He Is Strong When I Am Weak

Bible Verses:

2 Corinthians 12:9 (NRSV)[9] But he said to me, "My grace is sufficient for you, for power is made perfect in weakness." So, I will boast all the more gladly of my weaknesses, so that the power of Christ may dwell in me.[10] Therefore I am content with weaknesses, insults, hardships, persecutions, and calamities for the sake of Christ; for whenever I am weak, then I am strong.

Philippians 4:13 (NIV) I can do all things through him who gives me strength.

Thoughts to Consider:

There's a myth going around in social circles—even well-intentioned Christian circles—that "God won't give you more than you can handle." Unfortunately, that quote rather misses the mark about what God promises us and puts some pretty unreasonable expectations in front of us. The truth from scripture is that God won't allow anything to separate us from His love, but it's because of His power and His strength that we withstand our trials. Many of us have a desire to "do it ourselves." We rely on ourselves more than is healthy, and sometimes God allows trials to push us past our limits to that very point where we give up control and say, "I can't do this, God, but You can." That's where God meets us: when we're on our knees, at our weakest, He can be our strength. The apostle Paul went through a lot of trials in his life. He was imprisoned, beaten, imprisoned some more, and he had a "thorn in his flesh" that he says was a constant reminder to not boast on his own strength. His letter to the church in Corinth reveals his perspective on these trials–that he delights in them because that is when he sees Christ's power the clearest. Delighting in trials? Let's talk about that.

Question for Mother to answer:

Have you ever heard the phrase, "God won't give you more than you can handle," or other sayings like it? What do you think when you hear that phrase?

Question for Daughter to answer:

Do you know anyone close to you (yourself included) who tends to be a "do it myself" kind of person? What kinds of challenges do they face?

Verses to explore together

- 2 Corinthians 12:1–10
- Colossians 1: 9–13
- Philippians 4:11–13

Discussion Questions together:

1. What other sayings about God's strength or letting Him be in charge do we know?

2. What kinds of things do we try to control or do ourselves that might be easier if we let God take control?

Closing Prayer:

Lord, thank You for Your power and Your strength. We know we can do all things through You and Your strength, not our own. Thank You for meeting us and carrying us when we are weak. Help us to not wait so long to ask for Your help. Amen.

Search me,
O God, and know my
heart, try me and know
my thoughts: and see
if there be any wicked
way in me, and lead
me in the way
everlasting

Psalm 139:23-24

Different

WE ARE *SUPPOSED* TO BE DIFFERENT.

My daughters have noticed that I have raised them differently than some other parents have raised their kids. They noticed they have different permissions and different rules than their peers. We have rules about Saturday night sleepovers, about social media, about television and movie viewing, about the language we use, about how we treat each other, and about how we treat those around us. There's been a fair amount of irritation (sometimes even frustration) over the years about those rules, and that's okay.

The Bible tells us we are to be *in* this world but not of it (John 17:11–19). We are to walk among our fellow earth persons, and we are to do so with grace and compassion and love, but we are set apart. We are chosen. We are called, redeemed, and loved by God and transformed into His likeness. When we've accepted Him as Lord of our lives, we are to be and act different. Our light— more specifically His Light—is to shine through our lives in a way that causes others to stop and say, "Why are you different? How do I get that light?" We are meant to live so that by our words and our actions, others are drawn to the saving love of Jesus Christ.

Reflect a bit on how you are different from nonbelievers around you. How are your standards, your actions, your expectations, and your words different? How do your actions shine God's light and love to others? Use this week to reflect on how to reflect God in your life.

Looking at the Heart

Bible Verses:

1 Samuel 17:7b (NRSV) For the Lord does not see as mortals see; they look on the outward appearance, but the Lord looks on the heart.

Matthew 6:21 (NRSV) For where your treasure is, there your heart will be also.

Psalm 119:11 (NIV) I have hidden your word in my heart that I might not sin against you.

Thoughts to Consider:

Have you ever heard phrases that mention the heart? We talk about our "heart's deepest desire," loving someone "with all our heart," hoping "with all our heart," "putting our heart" into the work we're doing, "pouring out our heart" to someone else, saying something "from the bottom of our heart," wondering if we "have the heart" to do something, "wearing our heart" on our sleeve, and some people use the phrase "cross my heart" as a way of asserting something is true. What's with all that talk about hearts? The Bible has plenty to say about the heart, too. In both Matthew and Luke, Jesus is quoted saying the greatest commandment is to "Love the Lord Your God with all your heart." We're encouraged as believers to store up the Word of God in our hearts–to memorize it and to hold God's Word as Truth. Then, Psalm 37 says if we delight in the Lord, He will give us the desires of our hearts. This makes all kinds of sense because when we're delighting in Him, our hearts will be focused on desires that align with His plan for our lives. Let's talk about our hearts.

Question for Mother to answer:

What phrases do you use that contain the word "heart"? When do you use them, and what do you mean by them?

Question for Daughter to answer:

Why do you think the heart is so important in our daily language and in the Bible? What does the heart mean to you?

Verses to explore together

- Psalm 37:4
- Psalm 139:23–24
- James 3:14–17
- Psalm 51:10
- Matthew 6:19–21
- Matthew 6:33
- Proverbs 4:23
- Matthew 5:8
- Luke 10:25–28,
- Matthew 22:34–40
- Proverbs 3:5

Discussion Questions together:

1. Pick one or two of the verses above to memorize today, then talk about which one you picked and why.

2. Proverbs 4:23 says all things flow from the heart. What do you suppose that means, and how does it apply to your life?

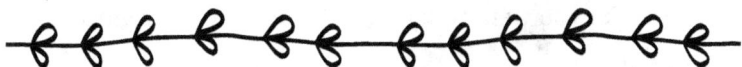

Closing Prayer:

Lord, thank You for creating our hearts. Thank You for teaching us to guard our hearts by filling them with Your word and Your love. Lord, help us to keep our hearts focused on You and Your glory so that Your light will shine in our lives. Amen.

My Body – A Temple

Bible Verses:

1 Corinthians 6:19–20 (NRSV) Or do you not know that your body is a temple of the Holy Spirit within you, which you have from God, and that you are not your own? For you were bought with a price; therefore glorify God in your body.

1 Corinthians 10:31 (NRSV) So, whether you eat or drink, or whatever you do, do everything for the glory of God.

Thoughts to Consider:

A temple is a dwelling place, usually associated with worship or reverence. In the Bible, "The Temple" generally refers to one of two buildings that were revered by the Jewish people as the holy places in which God dwells–the first built by King Solomon (1 Kings 6, 2 Chronicles 3) and the second being the Temple in Jerusalem where Jesus taught (Luke 21:37). The Temple was to be kept clean, holy, and pure, and Jesus overturned tables and drove out the money changers who had made the Temple something less clean than it should have been (Matthew 21). A Temple is a place of worship–a place where God dwells. What does that mean then for our body to be a temple of the Holy Spirit? What does that mean for the food we eat, things we see and read, the clothes we wear, the way we think of our bodies, and how we treat our bodies? Let's talk about our bodies as temples for a few minutes.

Question for Mother to answer:

What can you share about any of the places of worship you've seen in your lifetime (churches, cathedrals, buildings that are considered holy spaces)? How does the space itself point to God?

Question for Daughter to answer:

If someone walked into your room or your family's house, how would they know you lived there? What signs would they see that you (or your family) "own" that space?

Verses to explore together

- Romans 12:1–2
- Philippians 1:20
- Matthew 5:14–16
- Acts 1:8
- Matthew 6:22–23

❋ · ❋ · ❋ · ❋ · ❋ · ❋ · ❋ · ❋

Discussion Questions together:

1. What does it mean to you to think of your body as a temple—that God dwells within us and that we are His? How might that impact the way we dress or move or the situations we find ourselves in?

2. 1 Corinthians 10:31 says we should do everything for the glory of God. What do you suppose "everything" means in that sentence? How do we do that on a day to day basis?

❋ · ❋ · ❋ · ❋ · ❋ · ❋ · ❋ · ❋

Closing Prayer:

Lord, thank You for leaving Your Holy Spirit to dwell within us so we can shine Your light to the world. Lord, we confess that sometimes we don't do everything in a way that would bring You glory, and we ask for Your forgiveness. Lord, help us to find ways each day to make sure our words, our thoughts, our actions, and our hearts point to You. Amen.

My Words Reflect Him

Bible Verses:

James 1:19 (NRSV) You must understand this, my beloved: let everyone be quick to listen, slow to speak, slow to anger.

Ephesians 4:29 (NRSV) Let no evil talk come out of your mouths, but only what is useful for building up, as there is need, so that your words may give grace to those who hear.

Thoughts to Consider:

Words, words, words. They have the ability to do so much good and so much harm. Spoken with truth and grace, they can build others up. Spoken with careful planning and in love, they can cause change in others. Spoken in haste or in anger, they can do tremendous damage. Years ago, my Mom taught an object lesson during a children's sermon in which she squeezed out a tube of toothpaste onto a plate, then asked the children to put the toothpaste back into the tube again. Of course they couldn't put the toothpaste back into the tube, and the point of the lesson was that once the words are out of our mouths, they can't be taken back or put away again. The Bible has lots to say about words and about how to make sure our words are building others up and not tearing down. Building on our desire to do everything for the glory of God, an important place to start is our words. How do we keep our words from harming others or from being a poor representation of God's light? Let's talk about the power of words.

Question for Mother to answer:

Can you share any times in which the words others shared built you up or inspired you to do something differently or better?

Question for Daughter to answer:

Can you share any stories of when you successfully held your tongue instead of speaking out in anger?

Verses to explore together

- Colossians 4:6
- 1 Timothy 4:12
- Hebrews 13:7
- Psalm 19:14
- Matthew 15:11
- 1 Peter 3:10
- Proverbs 21:23
- Psalm 119:171–172
- Proverbs 18:20–21
- Proverbs 17:27–28
- Proverbs 12:18–19
- Proverbs 15:1–2

Discussion Questions together:

1. What's your favorite kind of toothpaste? Why?

2. Pick a verse to memorize today and talk about why you picked that one.

3. Are there any occasions where we spoke in anger or let words that were not uplifting come out of our mouths? What can we learn from those moments?

Closing Prayer:

Lord, thank You for loving us and for blessing us with the power of words. We confess that sometimes we aren't careful about what comes out of our mouths, and we do harm rather than shining Your light. Lord, this day, help us tame our tongues so that only what is good and right and uplifting to others comes out, so that we can continue to shine Your light to those around us. Amen.

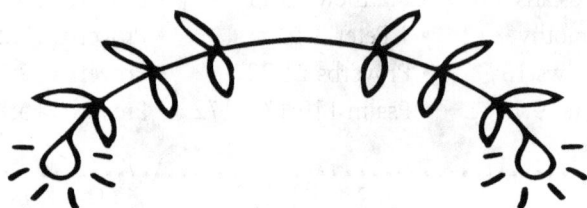

Love the Lord
your God with all
your heart and
with all your soul
and with all
your mind

Matthew 22:37 (NIV)

A Renewing of the Mind

Bible Verses:

Romans 12:2 (NRSV) Do not be conformed to this world, but be transformed by the renewing of your minds, so that you may discern what is the will of God— what is good and acceptable and perfect.

Philippians 4:8 (NRSV) Finally, beloved, whatever is true, whatever is honorable, whatever is just, whatever is pure, whatever is pleasing, whatever is commendable, if there is any excellence and if there is anything worthy of praise, think about these things.

Thoughts to Consider:

Have you ever had a really vivid nightmare? Or have you watched a scary movie or read a description in a book that was really gory or gross and then had trouble getting it out of your mind? Have you ever been part of a conversation that seemed to just go down-hill with negative talk and complaining or being mean and you had a hard time pulling yourself out of the conversation? How about those moments of self-talk where destructive thoughts start churning in our minds, criticizing the way we look or reminding ourselves of some way we think we're not as good as someone else? Ever had one of those moments? These thoughts can be pretty destructive, and they can rob us of our joy. But God didn't intend for us to dwell on things that bring us down. Remember, He came that we would have life and have it *abundantly!* One way to protect ourselves is to be careful what we allow to enter into our thoughts by way of our ears or our eyes. Remember the Sunday School song, "Oh be careful little eyes what you see"? Another way to protect our thoughts is to make a list of things that meet the description of Philippians 4:8 and have that ready so we can stop the negative and shift to the positive. Let's talk about these approaches.

Question for Mother to answer:

Are there any movies you've seen or books you've read that you wish you could un-see or un-read? How did you protect yourself from the next time?

Question for Daughter to answer:

Do you remember the song, "Oh be careful little eyes what you see"? If you can't sing it, Google it and play it on your phone. What does it mean to you?

Verses to explore together

- Luke 11:34
- Proverbs 15:26
- Isaiah 26:3

- Colossians 3:2
- 1 Peter 1:13
- Ephesians 4:20-25

- Colossians 3:2
- Romans 8:5-6
- Philippians 4:6-7

Discussion Questions together:

1. What are some other Sunday School songs we remember singing at Vacation Bible School or in Sunday School?

2. Let's compare lists of things that meet Philippians 4:8's description.

Closing Prayer:

Lord, thank You for giving us clear instructions for how to focus our minds on You. Sometimes we let ourselves churn in negative thoughts or conversations or allow ourselves to see and hear things that don't bring You glory. Help us focus our eyes and ears and minds on You and on things that are good. Amen.

When
I am afraid,
I put my trust
in you

Psalm 56:3 (NIV)

No Fear

Bible Verses:

Joshua 1:9 (NRSV) I hereby command you: Be strong and courageous; do not be frightened or dismayed, for the Lord your God is with you wherever you go.

Psalm 46:1–2 (NRSV) [1]God is our refuge and strength, a very present help in trouble. [2]Therefore we will not fear, though the earth should change, though the mountains shake in the heart of the sea.

Thoughts to Consider:

Someone said that the message, "Do not be afraid," shows up in the Bible 365 times. That seems like a handy "reminder-a-day" way for God to put our minds at ease in Him. Some people have a fear of spiders or snakes; other people fear crowds or being alone; still others are afraid of the dark or afraid of the future. There are plenty of Biblical characters who had a right to be afraid. Noah spent 40 days in a boat with a bunch of animals while the world flooded around him. Moses was stopped at the edge of the Red Sea with the Egyptian army closing in behind him. Esther needed to talk to the king, but he could have put her to death if she displeased him. Daniel was put in a den with hungry lions. Jonah got caught up in a fierce storm when he tried to run from God's instruction and then spent a couple of days in the belly of giant fish. Mary was pregnant out of wedlock. The disciples were in a boat with a raging storm around them while Jesus was asleep. Peter was asked to walk on water. Mary Magdalene was scared to find Jesus' body gone from the tomb. But in all of these scenarios, God was with them. They did not have to be afraid because God's hand of mercy and protection and direction and love was upon them. And some of them had some pretty astounding outcomes. They may have been weak and scared on their own, but through God, they needed to have no fear. Let's talk about fear.

Question for Mother to answer:

What kinds of things are you afraid of?

Question for Daughter to answer:

What do you do when you're afraid?

Verses to explore together

- 1 John 4:18
- Matthew 14:22–33
- Psalm 23:4
- Philippians 4:11-13
- Psalm 56:3
- Isaiah 43:1
- Isaiah 41:10
- 2 Timothy 1:7
- Isaiah 35:3-4

Discussion Questions together:

1. What other Bible stories do we know about people who might have been afraid? How did God work through the moment?

2. Pick a verse about fear to memorize today and share why you chose it. How can we share that verse with someone else so they can be reassured in a time of fear as well?

Closing Prayer:

Lord, thank You for Your promise to be with us so that we do not need to fear. Sometimes we're afraid anyway. Forgive us for our fear and help us to rely fully on You. Let our faith in You shine a light of hope for others so they may come to know You. Amen.

Have I not commanded you? Be strong and courageous. Do not be frightened and do not be dismayed, for the Lord your God is with you wherever you go

Joshua 1:9 (NRSV)

What Love Looks Like

Bible Verses:

1 Corinthians 13: 4–8a (NRSV) [4]Love is patient; love is kind; love is not envious or boastful or arrogant [5]or rude. It does not insist on its own way; it is not irritable or resentful; [6]it does not rejoice in wrongdoing, but rejoices in the truth. [7]It bears all things, believes all things, hopes all things, endures all things. [8]Love never ends.

Thoughts to Consider:

It's been said that love is more than a feeling. It's a set of actions and words that demonstrate that feeling. Love is a verb more than it is a noun. For some of us, patience is really, really, really hard, but love means being patient anyway. Love means putting someone else first. Love means not insisting we have it our way. Love means delighting in what is true. Love means forgiving, even when it feels easier to hold a grudge. Love means wanting what's best for the other person even more than we want what's best for ourselves. God loves us and wants a personal relationship with us, but we keep making mistakes over and over again, and He loves us anyway. He's patient with us as we have grouchy days and unkind days and selfish moments. God even shows us that love means giving up your very life for another to save them. That's hard for us to imagine on a day-to-day basis. Let's talk about showing love.

Question for Mother to answer:

Can you think of a time when you have showed love, even when it cost you or meant putting your own needs aside for that other person?

Question for Daughter to answer:

What do you do to show love at home to your parents or your siblings or your pets, or at school or work with your friends?

Verses to explore together

- 1 Corinthians 13:1–13
- 1 Peter 4:8
- Colossians 3:12-14
- 1 John 3:16
- John 15:13

Discussion Questions together:

1. Our way of understanding and expressing love grows over time. How has your understanding of what love looks like changed over time?

2. One exercise is to live out 1 Corinthians 13:4–6 by replacing the word "love" with your name as a way to form new habits. For example: "(Name) is patient; (Name) is kind; (name) is not envious or boastful or arrogant or rude…." How might we apply that today or this week?

Closing Prayer:

Lord, thank You for Your love. Thank You for showing us what love looks like and giving us more and more examples in our lives so that we can continue to grow in our understanding of Your love. Help us to help others see love by living love today. Amen.

Love is patient, love is kind

1 Corinthians 13:4 (NIV)

I've Got the Joy, Joy, Joy, Joy

Bible Verses:

Philippians 4:4 (NRSV) Rejoice in the Lord always; again I will say, Rejoice.

Psalm 118:24 (NRSV) This is the day that the Lord has made; let us rejoice and be glad in it.

Philippians 2:14 (NIV) Do everything without grumbling or arguing.

Thoughts to Consider:

Let's face it, not all situations seem joy-inducing. As humans, we don't always feel the joy. Cleaning bathrooms? Doing homework? Paying bills? Separating kids who are fighting with each other? Getting interrupted when trying do something for ourselves to go take care of something for someone else. Cleaning sticky-spilled-caked-on-goo off the inside of the microwave or the fridge shelf or the floor again. Um, these are not exactly everyone's favorite things. But the Psalmist and Paul both write about being, feeling, and showing joy *all* the time. You see, it's an example of the Fruit of the Spirit. That means if the Lord is dwelling in our hearts, and we have His Spirit within us, we can't help but be joyful, just as we can't help but feel love in the presence of Love defined. In all circumstances, we should rejoice. Paul writes, "Rejoice always," and then he says it again: "Again, I say, rejoice." We've talked about Paul and how he had a right to be full of fear or to complain about his circumstances, but he wasn't and he didn't. When Paul wrote to the church in Philippi that they needed to "do everything without grumbling or arguing," it was behavior he was modeling for them. Let's talk about rejoicing and doing things without grumbling.

Question for Mother to answer:

Share a story about when you grumbled about something and it caused a chain of events (like dominoes falling) that stole joy from the moment.

Question for Daughter to answer:

What's likely to make you grumble? If you had a "grumble jar" where you had to pay a fine if you were caught grumbling, how full would it be?

Verses to explore together

- Psalm 47:1
- 1 Peter 1:8–9
- Nehemiah 8:10
- Romans 15:13
- Psalm 30:5
- Philippians 4:4
- 1 Thessalonians 5:16
- Psalm 32:11

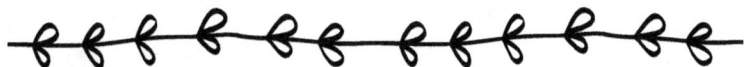

Discussion Questions together:

1. What do our faces look like or our words sound like when we are showing joy?

2. What are some of the most joy-filled moments we've shared together?

Closing Prayer:

Lord, thank You that You are our joy. Thank You for providing us with an unending supply of reasons to rejoice. Forgive us when we forget to keep counting our blessings and instead start listing reasons to grumble or complain. Help us fix our eyes on You and be filled with Your joy so we may draw others to the joy only You can provide. Amen.

Come to me,
all you who are
weary and burdened,
and I will give
you rest

Matthew 11:28 (NIV)

WEEK FOUR

Rest

REST IS GOOD.

In our frenetic and busy lives today, we have way too much going on. We have timers for our timers and reminders for our reminders. We have schedules that are so chock-full, that many of us struggle to even schedule in bathroom breaks!

And women seem to bear a whole lot of society-inflicted (and sometimes self-inflicted) stress. Many of those who spend their waking hours tending to the household sometimes set the bar pretty high for themselves in terms of how obedient the children are, how clean things are, how well-decorated the house is for the current season, how home-made the birthday treats are, how closely their homes or lives match the Pinterest boards or the Facebook posts of the experts (or their neighbors). Many of us have jobs outside the home, and with the rise of women in the workforce and two-career families, it's been said that women today are expected to bring home the bacon, fry it up, serve it up, clean it up, and then run it off on the treadmill. Phew–that's exhausting! We need a break or a vacation or at least a chance to rest.

What could possibly be a better way to demonstrate rest than to set aside, intentionally and consistently, a few minutes of quiet, restful conversation about God?

I pray that through this devotional workbook, you have a chance to build habits of stopping and resting in God's goodness. Rest in the confidence that He will sustain you, and He will shelter you, and He will provide for you. Rest in the knowledge that He leads you beside still waters, and He restores your soul.

Use this week to reflect a bit on your daily schedule. How will you deliberately create time to rest in God?

Peace Like No Other

Bible Verses:

Isaiah 26:3 (NLT) You will keep in perfect peace all who trust in you, all whose thoughts are fixed on you!

John 14:27 (NRSV) Peace I leave with you; my peace I give to you. I do not give to you as the world gives. Do not let your hearts be troubled, and do not let them be afraid.

Thoughts to Consider:

Did you see it? "Perfect peace." During the Christmas season, we talk a lot about "peace on earth," and there are several groups committed to world peace or peace in certain troubled regions, but personal peace? That's not something we talk about much. And *perfect* peace, wow, that's seems hard to come by. We are so caught up in the ever-busy pace of our day-to-day lives, the constant hum of technology, the ever-present ping and ding of notifications of calls received, messages to read, posts to respond to, timers going off, and things to do.

It's no wonder our stress levels are so high! When do we get peace? When do we get quiet? Ever heard the one about the little girl who proudly served her parents a bag of frozen peas and carrots for an early Saturday morning breakfast in bed, declaring "Mom and Dad, I made just what you asked for this morning 'Peas and Quiets'!" Is there a place or a scene that brings you peace? For some it's the calming effect of water; for others, it's an open view from a mountaintop. For some, it's a break from school or work; for others, it's a quiet evening with loved ones. But God promises perfect peace. No anxiety, no worries, no stress, no fear, no troubles, no hot-buttons, and no triggers that can set us off like a firecracker. Trust in Him. Focus on Him. Stay your mind on Him, and He grants *perfect* peace. Let's talk about peace.

Question for Mother to answer:

Think back to a time when you were "at peace" about some-thing–maybe a decision or a test or a big event. What put you "at peace"?

Question for Daughter to answer:

Where is a place (real or imagined) that gives you peace? Describe it in as much detail as you can.

Verses to explore together

- Philippians 4:5–7
- 1 Peter 5:7
- Psalm 29:11
- Colossians 3:15

❀ ∙ ∙ ❀ ∙ ∙ ❀ ∙ ∙ ∙ ❀ ∙ ∙ ∙ ❀ ∙ ∙ ❀ ∙ ∙ ❀ ∙ ∙ ∙ ❀

Discussion Questions together:

1. What are some of the specific things that disrupt your peace?

2. What steps can we take to contribute to peace for those around us?

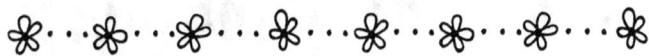

❀ ∙ ∙ ❀ ∙ ∙ ❀ ∙ ∙ ∙ ❀ ∙ ∙ ∙ ❀ ∙ ∙ ❀ ∙ ∙ ❀ ∙ ∙ ∙ ❀

Closing Prayer:

Lord, thank You for Your promise of peace—a peace that is perfect and that exceeds our understanding. Thank You for showing us examples of peace and for helping us fix our eyes on You. Lord, this day, help us know peace in You. Help us stay alert for ways we can help others find their peace in You, too. Amen.

Trust in
the Lord with
all your heart and
lean not on your
own understanding;
in all your ways
acknowledge him
and he shall
direct your
paths

Proverbs 3:5-6 (NKJV)

Trusting in Him

Bible Verses:

Proverbs 3:5–6 (NKJV) [5]Trust in the Lord with all your heart, and lean not on your own understanding; [6]In all your ways acknowledge Him, and He shall direct your paths.

Thoughts to Consider:

Have you ever felt just sure you had the right answer? You were so confident in your own knowledge or approach or insights that there was No. Possible. Way. you were wrong? Have you ever had that same sense of certitude and been, well, wrong? That's because we're human. We're prone to mistakes; they don't call it "human error" for nothing! Sometimes we look at situations in front of us, and they don't make sense. Maybe it's something bad that's happened or an answer to prayer that feels more like an unwarranted "no" than we'd planned. It turns out when we rely on our own finite perspective of what lies ahead, we can't see things the

way God sees them. He is omniscient (all-knowing) and omni-
present (in all places), and He goes before us and behind us and
walks beside us. If we trust in His wisdom and follow His direction, we can be absolutely confident that He will guide our steps
and take us in the direction He wants for us.

Question for Mother to answer:

Can you share a story about a time when you thought you
were right about something or someone or how a certain
thing should go, but then God revealed a path that was wiser
than your own thoughts?

Question for Daughter to answer:

What's one of those topics you're pretty sure about? How have
you learned or gained your knowledge in that topic?

Verses to explore together

- Psalm 146:3–6
- Proverbs 28:26
- Psalm 13:5–6
- Psalm 9:10
- Psalm 20:7
- Psalm 31:14
- Psalm 56:3
- Psalm 84:12
- Romans 15:13

Discussion Questions together:

1. Share stories about any time you've ever been part of (or observed) a "trust fall" or a trust-building climbing adventure.

2. What concrete actions can we take to demonstrate that we trust in the Lord?

Closing Prayer:

Lord, thank You that we can trust in You. Thank You for Your everlasting, unchanging, unfailing and boundless love for us. Thank You that You can see well beyond the next turn and that You already know all of our days. Lord, help us trust You more readily, more willingly, and help us to not rely on our own wisdom but rely on Your Word so others may see that we trust in You and also put their trust in You. Amen.

In Everything Give Thanks

Bible Verses:

Psalm 92:1 (NRSV) It is good to give thanks to the Lord, to sing praises to your name, O Most High.

1 Thessalonians 5:18 (NRSV) Give thanks in all circumstances; for this is the will of God in Christ Jesus for you.

Thoughts to Consider:

We've talked about Paul and some of the tough spots he was in, but let's spend a moment on David. When David wrote Psalm 57, he was hiding out in a cave, having already been anointed as King (1 Samuel 16), but having undergone repeated bouts of being hunted by Saul. In the midst of this dark moment (literally, he was in a cave), Psalm 57 shows David going back and forth between crying out to God in his despair and praising and thanking God for His goodness. He begins by pointing out the tough spot he's in and then calling on God's mercy, love, and faithfulness (vs 1–3). He goes on to describe how he feels surrounded by attackers (vs 4) and returns to glorifying God (vs 5). He describes how he feels trapped and ensnared (vs 6) but reminds himself that his heart is steadfast toward God (vs 7). He finishes with a song of praise, exalting God above all the earth (vs 8–11). Have you ever felt torn like that–listening to voices of despair and fighting back with words of praise? It's really easy for us to get caught up in the direness or the negative aspects of our current situations. We can become quickly overwhelmed by our circumstances even when they're not all that dire. As Americans, for example, we spend a whole lot of time griping about what some folks refer to as "first world problems." But if we train ourselves to give thanks to God, we can use those words of thanksgiving to focus on Him instead of on whatever it is we don't like about the given moment. Psalm 57 gives us some great tips to use to remind ourselves of God's goodness and steadfastness and His love for us, even in the dark moments of our lives. Let's talk about self-talk and then explore some of the verses about giving thanks.

Question for Mother to answer:

Can you share a story about when you were able to use positive words and a positive message to overcome words of fear or anguish?

Question for Daughter to answer:

What kinds of things can make you feel like you're trapped in a cave by someone who's out to get you?

Verses to explore together

- Psalm 57
- 1 Chronicles 16:34
- Psalm 28:7 (NRSV)
- Psalm 100:4

- Hebrews 13:15
- Ephesians 5:18–20
- Psalm 9:1
- Psalm 107:1

- Philippians 4:6–7
- Psalm 37:4
- Psalm 7:17
- Psalm 106:1

Discussion Questions together:

1. What are some of the nuisances in our lives that we let get under our skin when we would be better off focusing on God?

2. Pick one of the verses above to memorize, and share why you chose it.

Closing Prayer:

Lord, You are worthy of all praise. Thank You for Your enduring faithfulness and for Your steadfast and unending love. Thank You for Your patience with us and for being at our sides through everything we experience. Lord, we confess that sometimes we get caught up in the negative and forget to trust in You. Thank You for giving us examples of people who fixed their eyes on You, even in the toughest of moments. Lord, help us continue to focus our eyes, and our hearts, and our minds on You. Amen.

Give thanks
to the Lord
for he is good

Psalm 107:1 (NIV)

We Are His Sheep

Bible Verses:

Psalm 100 (NRSV) [1]Make a joyful noise to the Lord, all the earth. [2]Worship the Lord with gladness; come into his presence with singing. [3]Know that the Lord is God. It is he that made us, and we are his; we are his people, and the sheep of his pasture. [4]Enter his gates with thanksgiving, and his courts with praise. Give thanks to him, bless his name. [5]For the Lord is good; his steadfast love endures forever, and his faithfulness to all generations.

Psalm 23 (NKJV) [1]The Lord is my shepherd; I shall not want. [2]He makes me to lie down in green pastures; He leads me beside the still waters. [3]He restores my soul; He leads me in the paths of righteousness For His name's sake. [4]Yea, though I walk through the valley of the shadow of death, I will fear no evil; For You are with me; Your rod and Your staff, they comfort me. [5] You prepare a table before me in the presence of my enemies; You anoint my head with oil; My cup runs over. ⁶Surely goodness and mercy shall follow me All the days of my life; And I will dwell in the house of the Lord Forever.

Thoughts to Consider:

God is often referred to as "the Good Shepherd." He tends to us; He provides for our every need; He seeks us out and brings us back when we go astray; He leads us to moments and spaces where we can rest. He refreshes us. He shows us the way we should go. He comforts us, cares for us, and directs our paths. Like sheep, we are utterly dependent on our Shepherd, and our obedience to Him is our offering of worship. When shepherds bring their sheep together for the night, they can mix in a pen or shelter with other sheep, and when their shepherd calls out to them in the morning, they hear his voice and follow him. Each sheep will follow its own shepherd's voice, even if many sheep and shepherds are mixed together. God calls to us, and we know His voice. We are His. He made us, and He chose us, and He calls to us, and we are His.

Of course, we would want to enter His gates with thanksgiving and enter His courts with praise. But sometimes, we're just too bone-weary. The work of keeping up with the chaos, busyness, and demands of life is too much for us to bear. Sometimes we try to run away from the chaos of our lives and wind up in a spot that makes

it hard to hear God's still small voice inside us. But He is with us. His rod and His staff are a comfort to us. Sometimes in our lives, He makes us lie down in green pastures. And He leads us beside still waters. He restores our souls. For years in advertising, women have been targeted for products that help us get away, that comfort us, or that give us a chance to rest and refresh (think bubble baths–"Calgon, take me away"–or days at the spa or massages or mani-pedi's). These are kind of like how we restore our soul. Let's talk about restoring our souls.

Question for Mother to answer:

What do you do to refresh, relax, de-stress, and unwind?

Question for Daughter to answer:

When have you encountered a level of stress or distress that made you want to escape to restore your soul?

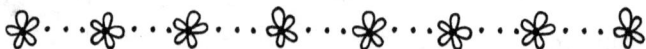

❀ · · ❀ · · ❀ · · · ❀ · · · ❀ · · · ❀ · · ❀ · · · ❀

Verses to explore together

- Psalm 23
- Psalm 100
- Psalm 46:10
- Psalm 37:3-8

❀ · · ❀ · · ❀ · · · ❀ · · · ❀ · · ❀ · · ❀ · · · ❀

Discussion Questions together:

1. What are a shepherd's rod and staff used for? If you're not sure, Google it.

2. Can you think of a time when you've seen God's hand helping you to stop, to lie down, and to rest? Share the story.

3. What habits or practices can we adopt that help us focus on the restoring of our soul that God does for us?

❀ · · ❀ · · ❀ · · · ❀ · · · ❀ · · ❀ · · ❀ · · · ❀

Closing Prayer:

Lord, thank you that we are Your sheep and that You love us and You care for us! Lord, in our lives sometimes we feel the many demands of what we're supposed to do, to such a degree that we forget to sometimes not do, but to stop, to be still, to know that You are God, that You've got this all in Your mighty hand, and that we can rest in You. Lord, help us follow where You lead so we might be restored and refreshed. Amen.

The Lord is
my shepherd,
I shall not want.
He makes me lie
down in green
pastures, he leads
me beside still
waters, He
restores my
soul

Psalm 23:1-3a (NRSV)

Making the Most of Our Talents

Bible Verses:

1 Peter 4:10 (NIV) Each of you should use whatever gift you have received to serve others, as faithful stewards of God's grace in its various forms.

Mark 8:26 (NIV) What good is it for someone to gain the whole world, yet forfeit their soul?

Thoughts to Consider:

Do you know a good gift giver—that person who always knows just what gift to give and wraps it beautifully? How about that woman who seems to always know just what to wear? How about that person who seems to always know just what to say? We know others, just as we become known, by consistent actions. The consistent habits we see in others help form our opinions of them. The way others consistently perceive us is how they remember us and how they talk about us to others. But what others see in us is not just a reflection on us and on our character; it is also a reflection on God, our heavenly Father. They say that integrity is doing the right thing even when no one is watching. God asks us to consistently and continually choose to do the thing that will bring Him glory. As Christians, we represent Him to those around us. Our actions, our words, where we invest our time and our money—these are all things that reflect on Him. So we should focus, then, on not winning the most trophies or earning the most dollars, or the most material possessions, or the best social status, or even the highest number of human friends or electronic "likes". Pursuing those things for their own sake runs counter to what God wants. He wants us to use the talents and gifts He's given us to shine His light to those around us. Did God grant you the ability to teach? Then teach His Word. Did God bless you with the gift of numbers or with the capability to connect with others? Did He give you a musical ear or an artistic eye? Are you gifted with an organized mind or the ability to give really great hugs? Then use those talents to help further His kingdom. Let's talk about talents.

Question for Mother to answer:

What are some ways you've put your God-given talents to work for His glory over the years?

Question for Daughter to answer:

What are some of your God-given talents?

Verses to explore together

- 1 Peter 4:10-11
- 1 John 2:17
- Matthew 6:19-21
- Matthew 16:24-27
- 2 Corinthians 7:1
- 1 Corinthians 13:1–3
- James 4:17
- Romans 12:3-8
- Ephesians 2:10

A good name is more desirable than great riches to be esteemed is better than silver or gold

Proverbs 22:1 (NIV)

❀ · · ❀ · · ❀ · · · ❀ · · · ❀ · · · ❀ · · · ❀ · · · ❀

Discussion Questions together:

1. Who are some of the people you both know who consistently point to God with their talents? How can you emulate them?

2. Sometimes doing the right thing or the thing that brings God glory isn't the easier path, but it's still the right path. What stories can you share about doing the right thing, even when it seems hard?

❀ · · ❀ · · ❀ · · · ❀ · · · ❀ · · · ❀ · · · ❀ · · · ❀

Closing Prayer:

Lord, thank You for Your many blessings. Thank You for granting to each of us unique skills and unique talents that we can use to serve You. Lord, sometimes we get caught up in our own selfish desires, trying to be the best for ourselves or to win the most for ourselves. Quiet our pride, and help us focus on using our talents to give You the glory. Amen.

How to "Be" Christian

Bible Verses:

Micah 6:8 (NRSV) He has shown all you people what is good. And what does the LORD require of you? To act justly and to love mercy and to walk humbly with your God.

John 13:34–35 (NRSV) [34]I give you a new commandment, that you love one another. Just as I have loved you, you also should love one another. [35]By this everyone will know that you are my disciples, if you have love for one another.

Thoughts to Consider:

A Christian is a follower of Christ or a person belonging to the faith of Christ. God made us in His image, and when we accept Him as Lord, His Holy Spirit dwells within us. So what does that mean in our daily lives? How do we behave? How do we "be" Christ-like in our daily lives. Today's devotional has us stopping for a bit to look at two different passages. One is from Paul's letter to the church at Philippi, and the other is found in the book of Hebrews. One of the great things about being a Christian is that we have the Bible, the holy and inerrant Word of God, to guide us and to serve as a lamp unto our feet and a light to our path (Isaiah 119:105). Both of the passages for today encourage the readers to follow Christ's example about how to "be" on a daily basis. Read them, pray over them, and let's talk about them.

Question for Mother to answer:

What do you do with recipes in the kitchen? Do you read them carefully and follow them closely, or are you more likely to "wing it"? Share some stories.

Question for Daughter to answer:

Think of construction toys, such as Legos, or other toys, games, or items you've had to assemble; how do you best go about understanding the instructions: reading, listening, talking, watching a video, seeing someone else, or trying it for yourself? What works best for you? Share some stories.

Verses to explore together

- Philippians 2:1–18
- Colossians 3:1-15
- Hebrews 12
- 1 Thessalonians 5:12-28
- Philippians 4:4-9

Discussion Questions together:

1. Imagine you're tasked, as a team, with helping someone else understand the gist of Hebrews 12. What are some of the key points you would share as instructions or guidelines for others?

2. Pick three ideas each that stand out to you from Philippians 2:1–18 and make a note of why they stand out. Compare your lists.

Closing Prayer:

Lord, thank You for setting the ultimate example of how to live and love like You. Thank You for surrounding us with a cloud of witnesses, both in Biblical times and in today's world, that we can look to as examples of how to be and live more like You. Lord, we know that when we fix our eyes on You, and when we seek You first, You will shine through our lives to Your glory. Lord, help us be more like You this day and each day from now on. Amen.

Putting Others Ahead of Ourselves

Bible Verses:

Philippians 2:4 (NRSV) Let each of you look not to your own interests, but to the interests of others.

John 13:34–35 (NRSV) [16]We know love by this, that he laid down his life for us—and we ought to lay down our lives for one another. [17]How does God's love abide in anyone who has the world's goods and sees a brother or sister in need and yet refuses help? [18]Little children, let us love, not in word or speech, but in truth and action.

Proverbs 19:17 (NRSV) Whoever is kind to the poor lends to the Lord, and will be repaid in full.

2 Corinthians 9:7 (NRSV) Each of you must give as you have made up your mind, not reluctantly or under compulsion, for God loves a cheerful giver.

Thoughts to Consider:

Have you heard the phrase, "I'm third"? What it refers to is putting God first, others second, and ourselves third. This is so counter to human nature that without divine intervention, it's pretty much impossible. Think about our current "me first" or "looking out for number one" kind of society. Society trains us to look out for ourselves–to grab what we can and push (or cut) to the head of the line. But that's not what God teaches us. God teaches us to put Him first and others second. The greatest commandments are Love God (First), and Love others (Second) (Matthew 22:36–40; Mark 12:28–31). Those aren't suggestions or hints or optional choices; they're commands. The Bible has a whole lot to say about how we can love our neighbor, be generous to others, and care for those in need. Let's talk about serving others.

Question for Mother to answer:

Very often, it's almost natural for us as mothers to put the needs of our children ahead of our own. Share some stories of how you see yourself doing that in your life.

Question for Daughter to answer:

Think of a time when you put someone else's needs ahead of your own. How did the story play out? Share the story and what you learned from it.

Verses to explore together

- Psalm 41:1–3
- Proverbs 11:24–25
- Philippians 2:3–4
- Romans 12:13
- Matthew 25:31-45

- Proverbs 22:9
- Proverbs 21:13
- 1 Timothy 6:17–19
- Hebrews 13:1–3

- Leviticus 25:35–37
- Deuteronomy 15:7–8
- Matthew 10:42
- James 1:27

❀ · · ❀ · · ❀ · · · ❀ · · ❀ · · · ❀ · · ❀ · · · ❀

Discussion Questions together:

1. Right here in our community, what are some of the opportunities we have to care for widows, orphans, or others in need?

2. Make an action plan to care for others together.

❀ · · ❀ · · ❀ · · · ❀ · · ❀ · · · ❀ · · ❀ · · · ❀

Closing Prayer:

Lord, thank You for loving us so that we can love others. Thank You for Your instructions on how to serve others and to put the needs of others ahead of our own. Lord, sometimes we get so caught up in our own lives that we forget to show hospitality or to show generosity or kindness to others. We forget to minister to those in need. Lord, help us this day to find ways to be Your hands and feet and to share Your love and mercy with those in need. Amen.

Our Daily Walk

Bible Verses:

Deuteronomy 4:39–40 (NRSV) [39]So acknowledge today and take to heart that the Lord is God in heaven above and on the earth beneath; there is no other. [40]Keep his statutes and his commandments, which I am commanding you today for your own well-being and that of your descendants after you, so that you may long remain in the land that the Lord your God is giving you for all time.

Colossians 2:6–7 (NRSV) [6]As you therefore have received Christ Jesus the Lord, continue to live your lives in him, [7]rooted and built up in him and established in the faith, just as you were taught, abounding in thanksgiving.

Psalm 119:105 (NRSV) Your word is a lamp to my feet and a light to my path.

Thoughts to Consider:

Imagine running a race of endurance. Not a sprint or something that will be over quickly, but a marathon or a cross-country race. What do you need to run a course like that? You probably need some training; a goal or a destination, for sure; definitely a map of the route and enough light to see the road. It might be nice to have some company or encouragement along the way to remind us to keep running. And we'd probably want to be free of distractions so we can focus on the race at hand. As we think about this analogy in terms of our daily walk with God, it might look something like this: We're firmly rooted in the knowledge of God's love and who He is and our Salvation–this is like our training. The goal is eternity with Him, and as Paul writes, "Forgetting what lies behind and straining forward to what lies ahead," we "press on toward the goal for the prize of the heavenly call of God in Christ Jesus" (Philippians 3:13–14). And as we run, we are surrounded by those who have faithfully run this course ahead of us so we can "run with endurance," by "fixing our eyes on Jesus" (Hebrews 12:1–2). And we know where to put each foot, because God has directed our steps because we trust in Him and give Him the glory (Proverbs 3:5–6). He lights the path with His Word (Psalm 119:105). Even better, because He goes with us, we don't have to worry one bit about tomorrow (Matthew 6:34) Let's talk about endurance races.

❃ · · ❃ · · ❃ · · · ❃ · · · ❃ · · ❃ · · ❃ · · · ❃

Question for Mother to answer:

Have you ever run a marathon (either literally or figuratively)? Share the story.

Question for Daughter to answer:

Have you ever had the chance to cheer someone else on at a literal or figurative marathon? Share the story.

Verses to explore together

- Matthew 6:34
- Philippians 3:13–14
- Isaiah 40:31
- Hebrews 12:1–2
- Ephesians 6:10–18

Discussion Questions together:

1. Whether you're a runner or not, talk about specific ways you can apply this running analogy to your daily walk with God.

2. Just as every athlete needs training and can benefit from the counsel of a coach and the encouragement of those around them, every Christian needs training and can benefit from the

counsel of a Christian adviser, friend, mentor, or coach and the encouragement of a "cloud of witnesses." Explore ways you can encourage each other on your daily walk.

Closing Prayer:

Lord, thank You for Your saving grace. Thank You for Your promise of eternity with You. Lord, as we spend each day trying to stay focused on You and on Your glory, let us not be distracted by worry. This day that You have made for us, let us be joyful, and thankful, and let us not be led off the path You have lit for us with Your Word. Lord, help us to encourage each other and to continue to fix our eyes on You. Amen.

This is the day that the Lord has made

Psalm 118:24 (NRSV)

Our Future

Bible Verses:

Jeremiah 29:11 (NRSV) For surely I know the plans I have for you, says the Lord, plans for your welfare and not for harm, to give you a future with hope.

Isaiah 54:10 (GNT) "The mountains and hills may crumble, but my love for you will never end; I will keep forever my promise of peace." So says the Lord who loves you.

Thoughts to Consider:

Have you ever thought it might be fun to be able to predict the future? It's pretty natural to want to know how things will turn out in the end, but our finite minds can't see into the future. We can look at our parents and grandparents to get a pretty good idea of what we might look like when we grow up. We can plan ahead for our education or our careers, though many of us today hold jobs that didn't even exist when we were kids. We don't know exactly what turns our lives will take, who we'll meet, or what impact we'll have on others. But we do know God has promised to be with us. We do know that we'll face trials and that God will carry us through. We do know He is eternal and unchanging; He was here before time began and He was, and He is, and He always will be. We know that He has demonstrated His Love for us and has made a way for our salvation and eternity with Him. We also know He has promised us hope, a future, and peace. He is the Lord of promises, and He has promised us a future with Him. Let's talk about the future.

Question for Mother to answer:

Share a story about any book you've read or movie you've seen about the future or time travel. How did the future in the work of fiction compare with the present in that same work of fiction?

Question for Daughter to answer:

What do you think life will be like when you have grandkids who are your age? What kinds of technology, inventions, or tools for transportation or communication do you imagine there will be?

Verses to explore together

- Philippians 4:19
- Romans 5:5
- Isaiah 41:10-13
- Philippians 1:6
- Mark 13:32
- Joshua 1:9
- Lamentations 3:21-23
- Matthew 6:25-34

Discussion Questions together:

1. Talk about your plans for the future. Think about some things you want to do together in the near future (within the next 1–3 months) and the distant future (sometime in the next 5–10 years).

2. Memorize Isaiah 54:10 (GNT) together. Create some sort of reminder (a note card, a sticker, a bookmark) to help you remember this verse each day.

Closing Prayer:

Lord, thank You that You love us, that You saved us, and that You've promised us a hope and a future. Lord, help us rest confidently in Your promise of peace, today and always. Amen.

But grow
in the grace
and knowledge
of our Lord and
Savior Jesus Christ.
To him be glory
both now and
forever!
Amen

2 Peter 3:18

What's Next?

Thoughts to Consider:

Thanks for making time to explore this 30-day devotional with me and with someone you love. I hope you found it useful and beneficial and that you had lots of chances to talk about your faith and about God and about how to follow Him together. The lessons will still be true next month and the month after that and the one after that. I encourage you to keep talking with one another, encouraging each other, and learning from each other. A second pass through the workbook will give you more time with the additional scripture verses and more time to color and doodle while you chat.

And now, I close with the words from Paul to the Ephesians:

Bible Verses:

Ephesians 3:14–21 (NRSV) [14]For this reason I bow my knees before the Father, [15]from whom every family in heaven and on earth takes its name. [16]I pray that, according to the riches of his glory, he may grant that you may be strengthened in your inner being with power through his Spirit, [17]and that Christ may dwell in your hearts through faith, as you are being rooted and grounded in love. [18]I pray that you may have the power to comprehend, with all the saints, what is the breadth and length and height and depth, [19]and to know the love of Christ that surpasses knowledge, so that you may be filled with all the fullness of God.

[20]Now to him who by the power at work within us is able to accomplish abundantly far more than all we can ask or imagine, [21]to him be glory in the church and in Christ Jesus to all generations, forever and ever. Amen.

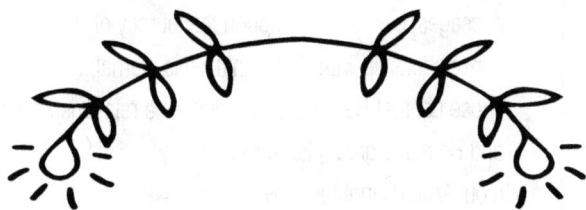

The End

Sample curriculum if you are doing this as a Sunday School or weekly Bible Study

DATE	TOPIC

Week 1	• Introduction to the Devotional Workbook and the structure
	• Week 1 messaging
	• Day 1 together
	• Put a plan in place for Day 2–7
	  o Messages 1–7 take us through the journey of our relationship with God – that He is eternal, that He chose us, that He sees us, He desires a relationship with us, and He has a great plan for us.
	  o In our Mom/Daughter conversations, we talk about eternity, love, being known, beauty, feeling unseen, relationships, and planning for the future.

Week 2	• Check-in as a group: What approaches are working for daily devotional time?
	• Week 2 messaging
	• Day 8 together
	• Small group discussion about learning so far: What have you learned?
	• Put a plan in place for Day 9–14
	  o Messages 8–14 take us through Romans Road to Salvation and explores God as a defender and a source of strength, even in tough times and moments of heartbreak and weakness.
	  o In our Mom/Daughter conversations, we talk about darkness, gifts, life-changing moments, games, and trials.

Week 3	• Check-in as a group: What's been hard?
	• Week 3 messaging
	• Day 15 together
	• Small group discussion about learning so far: What have you learned?
	• Put a plan in place for Day 16–21
	o Messages 15–21 take us through God's view of our hearts, our bodies, our words, our minds, and our strength, as well as the fruit of the spirit.
	o In our Mom/Daughter conversations, we talk about our hearts, our bodies, our words, our eyes, fear, ways to show love, and the effects of grumbling.
Week 4	• Check in as a group: What habits are you forming? What has delighted you?
	• Week 4 messaging
	• Day 22 together
	• Small group discussion about learnings so far: what have you learned?
	• Put a plan in place for Days 23–28
	o Messages 22–28 take us through peace, trust, thanksgiving, our Lord the Good Shepherd, being Christ-like, and loving others.
	o In our Mom/Daughter conversations, we talk about being right, learning, using words to lift others up, rest, talents, building things, and putting others' needs first.

Week 5	• Check in as a group: What will you sustain from here?
	• Day 29 together
	• Small group discussion about how you will apply what you've learned.
	• Put a plan in place for Day 30 and "What's Next"
	  o Messages 28–30 talk about our daily walk and our future with God.
	  o In our Mom/Daughter conversations, we talk about running and time travel.
	• Wrap-up

About the Author

Sinikka Waugh, President and Founder of Your Clear Next Step, spends her days teaching people to have better workplace interactions, praying that through her relentless positivity, grace-filled teaching, and firm commitment to the Gospel, that others will see and be drawn closer to Christ. Sinikka is a Rotarian and is consistently active in the faith community, including hosting an annual women's retreat in the Fall in Warren County, leading worship on Sunday mornings at her church, and writing and leading Bible studies.

Sinikka holds a BA from Central College, an MA from the University of Iowa, and is a certified Project Management Professional through the Project Management Institute (PMI). Sinikka and her husband Spencer live in Indianola, Iowa with their two teenage daughters, and two garage cats that have made their way into the family's hearts, even though the whole family is allergic.

Izdavačko preduzeće
RAD
Beograd, Dečanska 12

*

Glavni urednik
NOVICA TADIĆ

*

Grafički urednik
MILAN MILETIĆ

*

Korektor
MIROSLAVA STOJKOVIĆ

*

Priprema teksta
Grafički studio RAD

*

Za izdavača
SIMON SIMONOVIĆ

*

Štampa
Elvod-print, Lazarevac

CIP – Каталогизација у публикацији
Народна библиотека Србије, Београд

159.964.2

Фројд, Сигмунд

    Đavolja neuroza : izabrani ogledi / Sigmund Frojd ; [izabrao i
preveo Jovica Aćin]. – Beograd : Rad, 2001 (Lazarevac : Elvod-print).
– 125 str. ; 20 cm. – (Reč i misao ; knj. 454)

ISBN 86-09-00375-2

a) Психоанализа

ID=39088652

www.ingramcontent.com/pod-product-compliance
Lightning Source LLC
Chambersburg PA
CBHW060910280326
41934CB00007B/1266